THE COMPLETE LIST OF US PRESIDENTS FROM 1789 TO 2016

US HISTORY KIDS BOOK
Children's American History

orty-four men have been President of the United States, from 1789 to 2016. Let's find out a little bit about them!

ELECTING A PRESIDENT

In the United States, citizens vote every four years for a president and vice-president. But they actually vote for "electors" who pledge to support one of the presidential candidates in the Electoral College. Each state has at least three electors, but states with large populations, like California, have many more. A candidate can win the most votes on election day but still not be president because the other candidate had more votes in the Electoral College.

From 1776, when it became independent, to 1789 the United States had a different system of government, and fourteen men served as president during that time.

However, we normally consider the "real" presidents to be those after the current Constitution came into effect. The first election under that Constitution was in 1788.

Presidents get elected in November of a year divisible by four (1788, 1782, and so on), but don't take office until early in the next year. So for most of the presidents below, their terms start in odd-numbered years.

CONSTITUTION TO CIVIL WAR

GEORGE WASHINGTON (1789-97)

Washington, the first president, was a hero of the American Revolution and highly popular across the country. He was the only president elected unanimously (all votes for him) in the Electoral College. Washington was elected twice. He could have been elected again, but he felt that eight years was enough for any person to be in charge.

JOHN ADAMS (1797-1801)

Adams had been Vice President under Washington, and was elected president when Washington did not run a third time. He had been a leader in the Revolution, but was not personally popular. He ran for a second term, but did not win.

THOMAS JEFFERSON (1801-09)

Jefferson was the main author of the Declaration of Independence. He served for two terms. Under him, the country expanded greatly by buying the Louisiana Territory from France.

JAMES MADISON (1809-17)

Under Madison, the United States fought the War of 1812 with Great Britain. At one point the President had to flee Washington when the British attacked it and burned the White House. The war ended in a treaty in 1815, and both sides claimed victory. He served two terms.

JAMES MONROE (1817-25)

During Monroe's two terms the country expanded and prospered, but tensions grew between the southern, slave-holding states and the states that had abolished slavery.

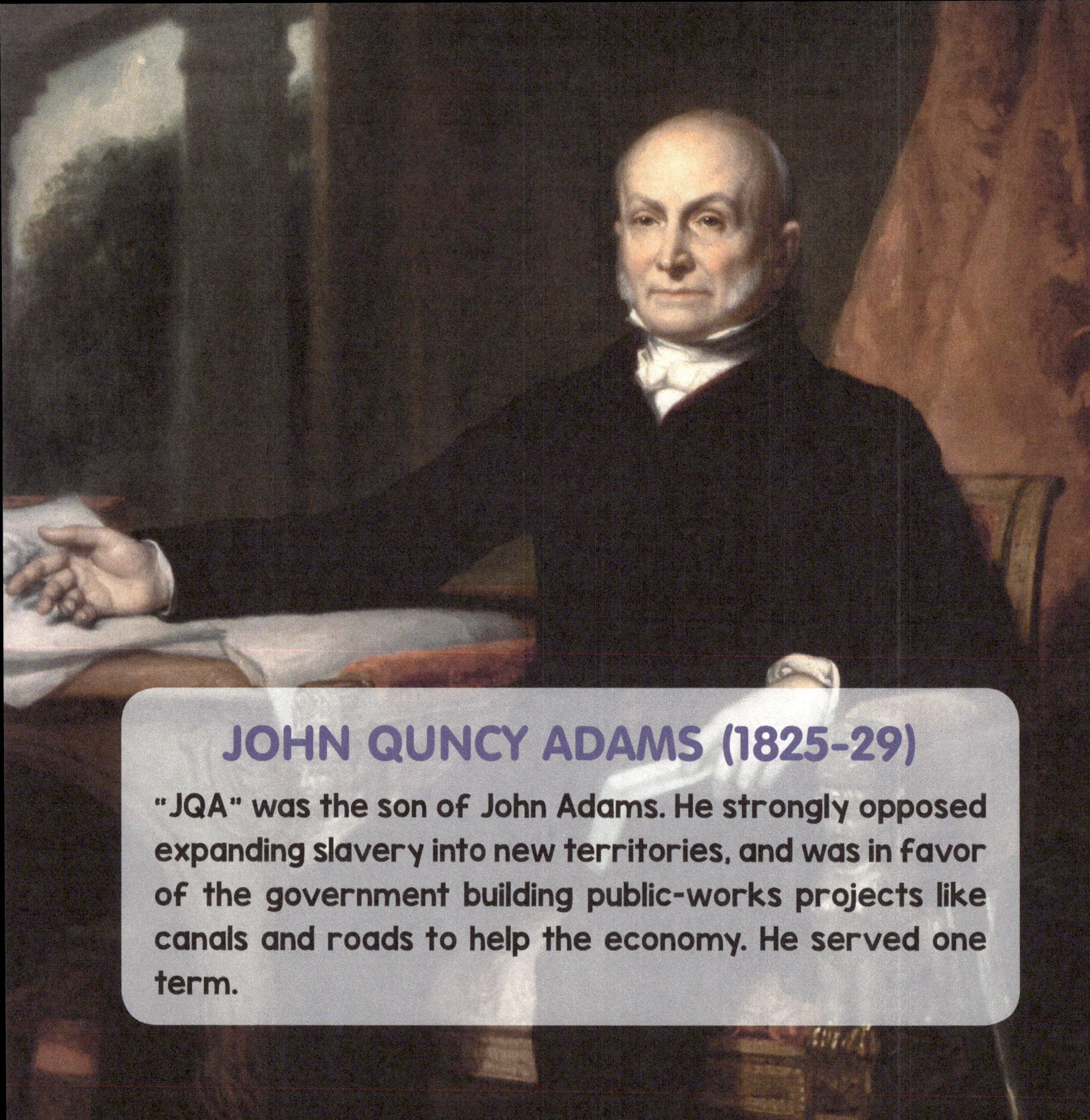

JOHN QUNCY ADAMS (1825-29)

"JQA" was the son of John Adams. He strongly opposed expanding slavery into new territories, and was in favor of the government building public-works projects like canals and roads to help the economy. He served one term.

ANDREW JACKSON (1829-37)

Jackson was a hero of the Indian Wars. He was strongly in favor of relocating Native Americans west so white Americans could take their land. Read more about this in the Baby Professor book The Heart-Shattering Facts about the Trail of Tears. He served two terms.

MARTIN VAN BUREN (1837-41)

Van Buren continued Jackson's policies concerning Native Americans. He made serious mistakes about the economy, so the financial crisis of 1837 lasted much longer than it could have. He served one term.

WILLIAM HENRY HARRISON (1841)

Harrison was a hero of the Indian Wars. He was sworn into office in a heavy rain, caught a chill, became very ill, and died one month later.

JOHN TYLER (1841-45)

Tyler, the Vice-President, became president and completed Harrison's term. He lowered tariffs to encourage international trade.

JAMES K. POLK (1845-49)

Under President Polk, who served one term, the United States gained the Oregon territory from Great Britain by treaty, and southwestern lands after winning the Mexican-American War.

ZACHARY TAYLOR (1849-50)

Taylor died during his term of office, which was marked by increasing tensions between slave and free states, and a huge movement west to hunt for gold in California.

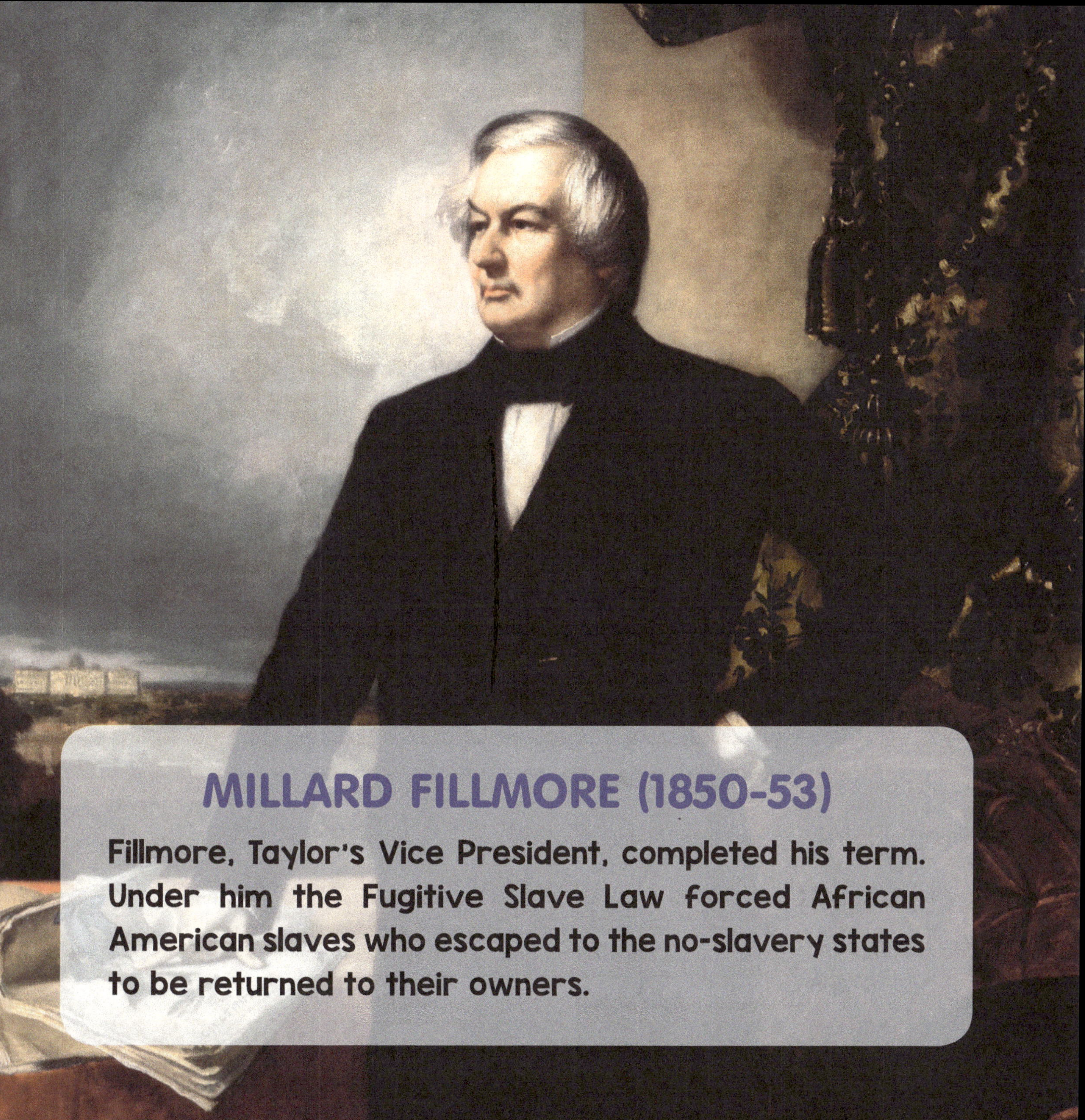

MILLARD FILLMORE (1850-53)

Fillmore, Taylor's Vice President, completed his term. Under him the Fugitive Slave Law forced African American slaves who escaped to the no-slavery states to be returned to their owners.

FRANKLIN PIERCE (1853–57)

Under Pierce, who served one term, the slave states pushed to expand slavery into the western territories. They threatened to leave the United States if they were not allowed to do this.

JAMES BUCHANAN (1857-61)

Buchanan tried to keep the country together, but was an ineffective leader. An economic crisis also hurt the country.

THE CIVIL WAR TO THE GREAT DEPRESSION

ABRAHAM LINCOLN (1861-65)

The southern states threatened that if Lincoln were elected and opposed expanding slavery, they would break up the country. After Lincoln became president, the Civil War began. During the war Lincoln issued the Emancipation Declaration that ordered the end of slavery. The slave-free North won the war after much grief and bloodshed. Lincoln was elected to a second term, but was shot and killed by a Southern loyalist just after the end of the war.

ANDREW JOHNSON (1865-69)

Johnson, the Vice President, completed Lincoln's term.
But he fought with Congress and the Senate almost voted
to remove him from office.

ULYSSES S. GRANT (1869-77)

Grant was a great Civil War general, and did some good works during his two terms in office. But his time is mainly remembered for corruption and scandals in his administration, and for financial crises.

RUTHERFORD B. HAYES (1877–81)

Hayes was elected by the Electoral College even though more people had voted for his opponent, Samuel Tilden. During this time supporters of slavery in the southern states started to roll back any advances African Americans had made after the Civil War. He served one term.

JAMES A. GARFIELD (1881)

Garfield was the second president to be assassinated. He was shot in September, 1881, and died a few weeks later.

CHESTER A. ARTHUR (1881-84)

Vice President Arthur became president and completed
one term. He tried to stop or control political corruption,
without much success.

GROVER CLEVELAND (1885–89)

Cleveland wanted to lower taxes on imported goods, so prices would be lower for consumers. This was unpopular with business interests, and he lost his attempt to be re-elected.

BENJAMIN HARRISON (1889-93)

During his single term, Harrison's government brought in a tariff (tax) act that disrupted the economy and caused economic trouble for farmers. His attempts to deal with a financial crisis were unpopular and unsuccessful.

GROVER CLEVELAND (1893-97)

Cleveland returned to office, but his administration was disrupted by the financial panic of 1893. He was opposed to efforts to expand United States territory into Central American and the Pacific Ocean. He is the only president to have served two terms with a gap in between.

WILLIAM MCKINLEY (1897-1901)

Under McKinley, who favored United States expansion, the nation annexed Hawaii and won the Spanish-American War. He won a second term in 1900, but was shot and killed in September, 1901.

THEODORE ROOSEVELT (1901-1909)

Roosevelt was hugely popular for his role in the Spanish-American War. He completed McKinley's term, and then was elected in his own right. Roosevelt did many ambitious things, including support for the Panama Canal, creating the National Parks system, and leading the country through an economic crisis.

WILLIAM HOWARD TAFT (1909-13)
Taft served one term, bringing in progressive policies to help poor and under-equipped people and communities, and breaking up huge corporations that were distorting the country's economy.

WOODROW WILSON (1913-1921)

During Wilson's two terms, the United States fought in what came to be known as the First World War. He helped negotiate the treaty ending the war, and helped establish the League of Nations as a place where countries could resolve differences peacefully. During his time in office, women gained the right to vote.

WARREN G. HARDING (1921-23)

Harding presided over a time when the automobile, film, and aviation industries were growing very quickly. But his administration was marred by financial scandals. He died of a heart attack part-way through his term.

CALVIN COOLIDGE (1923-29)

Coolidge, the Vice President, completed Harding's term and then won re-election. During his term the economy grew faster than could be sustained.

HERBERT HOOVER (1929-33)

While Hoover was president, the stock market collapsed and the national and world economies went into a steep decline. Hoover was unable to find solutions, and left office after a single term.

NEW DEAL
TO TODAY

Roosevelt signing TVA Act (1933)

FRANKLIN D. ROOSEVELT (1933-1945)

Roosevelt was elected four times, and served longer than any other president. He steered the country through recovery from the Great Depression, and then to victory in World War II. He also brought in many programs, now known as the "New Deal", to help people who fall on hard times. He suffered from polio and other ailments, and died in office before the end of World War II.

HARRY S. TRUMAN (1945-1953)

Truman, the Vice President, completed Roosevelt's term and then was elected once himself. He presided over the post-war recovery of the economy, victory in the Korean War, and the founding of the United Nations. He ordered desegregation of the armed forces.

DWIGHT D. EISENHOWER (1953–61)
Eisenhower was a general in World War II. During his two terms there was a huge scare about communist spies in the United States, the start of the space race, and a prosperous economy.

JOHN F. KENNEDY (1961-63)

Under Kennedy, the United States forced the Soviet Union to withdraw missiles from Cuba and to end a blockade of Berlin, the former German capital. He ordered an increase of U.S. troops fighting in Vietnam. He was shot and killed in 1963.

LYNDON BAINES JOHNSON
(1963-1969)

Vice President Johnson completed Kennedy's term and then was elected himself. He pressed for desegregation of schools and other institutions in the southern states, and for greatly increased social programs. He also presided over a hugely-unpopular war effort in Vietnam, and decided not to try to be re-elected.

RICHARD NIXON (1969-74)

Nixon presided over the end of the Vietnam War, better relations with China, and a time of social unrest. He was forced to resign after his second election in a political scandal.

GERALD FORD (1974-77)
Ford had been appointed Vice President to replace Spiro Agnew who resigned because of a scandal. He then completed Nixon's term as President.

JIMMY CARTER (1977-81)
During Carter's time in office, there was an economic crisis and threats of wars. He served one term.

RONALD REAGAN (1981-1989)
During his two terms, Reagan moved U.S. policies in a
more conservative direction. He also improved relations
with the Soviet Union.

GEORGE BUSH (1989-93)
Reagan's Vice President was elected president for one term. He led the country through the Persian Gulf War.

BILL CLINTON (1993-2001)

Clinton was elected to two terms, though we was also almost voted out of office by the Senate because of a scandal. His policies favored women and minority rights, and helped the economy.

GEORGE W. BUSH (2001-09)

The son of the first President Bush was elected twice, both times under conditions that led many people to claim fraud. The U.S. suffered its worst terrorist attack, known now as 9-11, during his term. He led wars in Afghanistan and Iraq.

BARACK H. OBAMA (2009-2017)
Obama was the first African American to be President. He ended the war in Iraq and reformed the U.S. health care system.

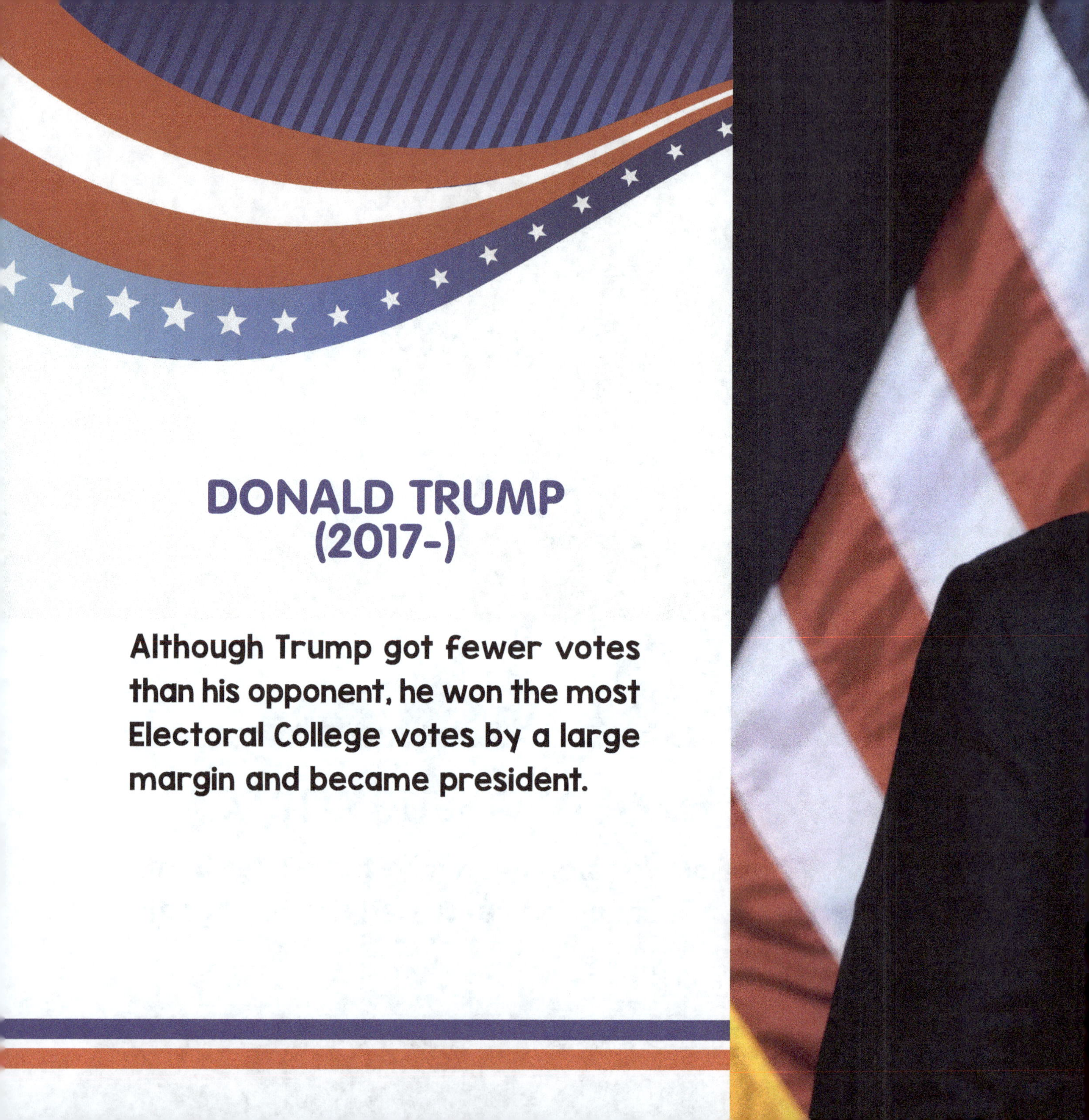

DONALD TRUMP
(2017-)

Although Trump got fewer votes than his opponent, he won the most Electoral College votes by a large margin and became president.

A GREAT NATION

Learn more United States history in Baby Professor books like King Philip's War and Marquis de Lafayette - Hero of Two Continents.

Visit
BABY PROFESSOR
EDUCATION KIDS
www.BabyProfessorBooks.com
to download Free Baby Professor eBooks
and view our catalog of new and exciting
Children's Books